M000248576

ALL AROUND THE WORLD
PANAMA

by Kristine Spanier, MLIS

pogo

Ideas for Parents and Teachers

Pogo Books let children practice reading informational text while introducing them to nonfiction features such as headings, labels, sidebars, maps, and diagrams, as well as a table of contents, glossary, and index.

Carefully leveled text with a strong photo match offers early fluent readers the support they need to succeed.

Before Reading

- "Walk" through the book and point out the various nonfiction features. Ask the student what purpose each feature serves.
- Look at the glossary together. Read and discuss the words.

Read the Book

- Have the child read the book independently.
- Invite him or her to list questions that arise from reading.

After Reading

- Discuss the child's questions. Talk about how he or she might find answers to those questions.
- Prompt the child to think more. Ask: What did you know about Panama before you read this book? What more would you like to learn?

Pogo Books are published by Jump!
5357 Penn Avenue South
Minneapolis, MN 55419
www.jumplibrary.com

Library of Congress Cataloging-in-Publication Data

Names: Spanier, Kristine, author.
Title: Panama / by Kristine Spanier, MLIS.
Description: Minneapolis, MN: Jump!, Inc., [2022]
Series: All around the world | Audience: Ages 7–10
Identifiers: LCCN 2020057710 (print)
LCCN 2020057711 (ebook)
ISBN 9781636900247 (hardcover)
ISBN 9781636900254 (paperback)
ISBN 9781636900261 (ebook)
Subjects: LCSH: Panama—Juvenile literature.
Classification: LCC F1563.2 .S63 2022 (print)
LCC F1563.2 (ebook) | DDC 972.87—dc23
LC record available at https://lccn.loc.gov/2020057710
LC ebook record available at https://lccn.loc.gov/2020057711

Editor: Jenna Gleisner
Designer: Molly Ballanger

Photo Credits: benedek/iStock, cover; jlazouphoto/iStock, 1; Mikrobiuz/Shutterstock, 3; BobHemphill/iStock, 4; Mellisandre/Dreamstime, 5; Wollertz/Shutterstock, 6-7tl; Damsea/Shutterstock, 6-7tr, 15; Slowmotiongli/Dreamstime, 6-7bl; Rich Carey/Shutterstock, 6-7br; Feathercollector/Dreamstime, 8-9; RIEGER Bertrand/Hemis/SuperStock, 10; Paulo Costa/iStock, 11; Rodrigo Cuel/Shutterstock, 12-13; FreezeFrameStudio/iStock, 14l; Dalaifood/Shutterstock, 14r; Stock Connection/SuperStock, 16-17; Gilberto Henriquez/Shutterstock, 18-19; M Guadarrama - SAMURAI JAPAN/Getty, 20-21; YamabikaY/Shutterstock, 23l; Echo 23 Media/Shutterstock, 23r.

Printed in the United States of America at Corporate Graphics in North Mankato, Minnesota.

TABLE OF CONTENTS

CHAPTER 1

LAND BRIDGE

Welcome to Panama! This country is in Central America. It is an **isthmus**. This land bridge lies between the Atlantic and Pacific Oceans. It connects North and South America.

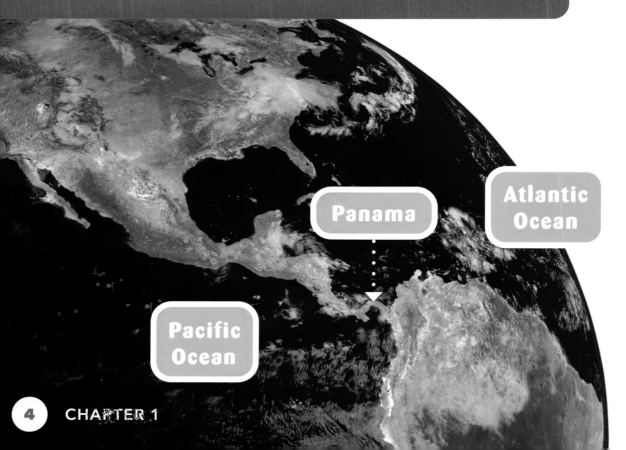

Atlantic Ocean

Panama

Pacific Ocean

The country's highest mountain is Volcán Barú. It is 11,398 feet (3,474 meters) tall. From it, you can see the sun rise over the Pacific Ocean. You can see it set over the Atlantic Ocean. This is the only place on Earth you can do this!

Over time, animals crossed the land bridge. Many different animals now live in Panama. Armadillos and sloths from South America live here. Jaguars and tapirs from North America live here. Giant sea turtles live near the coast.

DID YOU KNOW?

More than 1,000 islands are part of Panama. The largest is Coiba Island. White-faced capuchin monkeys live here. They use stones to open shells and coconuts!

armadillo

sloth

tapirs

sea turtle

harpy eagle

Panama's **climate** is **tropical**. A rain forest is in Darién **National** Park. It rains up to 180 inches (457 centimeters) a year here. Harpy eagles nest in trees.

WHAT DO YOU THINK?

There are nearly 1,000 bird **species** in Panama. The harpy eagle is the national bird. Does your country have a national bird? What is it?

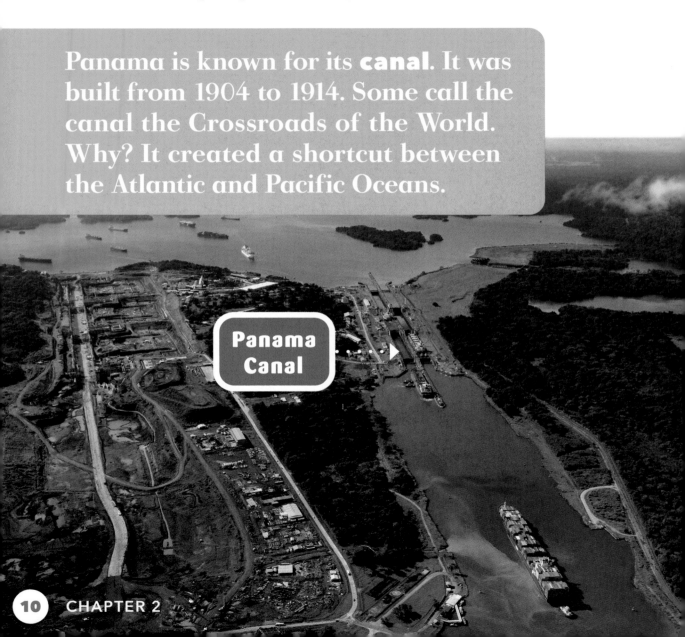

CHAPTER 2

BUSY CANAL

Panama is known for its **canal**. It was built from 1904 to 1914. Some call the canal the Crossroads of the World. Why? It created a shortcut between the Atlantic and Pacific Oceans.

Panama Canal

Before the canal was built, ships had to go around the southern tip of South America. Trips took many months. Now, they take 10 hours! Ships are able to move **goods** faster.

Panama City

Panama City is nearby. It is Panama's largest city. It is also the **capital**. The government meets here.

WHAT DO YOU THINK?

Panama's president serves for five years. The president of the United States serves for four years. How many years do you think a president should be able to serve? Why?

CHAPTER 3
LIFE IN PANAMA

A favorite meal here is arroz con pollo. This is rice with chicken. Chicha is a drink. It is made with pineapple, sugar, and water.

arroz con pollo

chicha ·····▶

Farmers grow **crops**. These include rice, bananas, coffee beans, pineapples, and sugarcane. They also raise **livestock**, such as cattle and hogs.

pineapple plants

Most children wear uniforms to school. They learn Spanish and English. In **rural** areas, schools may be far away. It is hard for children to get to them. They may help their families farm instead.

The **Festival** of the Pollera takes place in Las Tablas. Women wear polleras. Some take longer than six months to make!

TAKE A LOOK!

What are the parts of a pollera called? Take a look!

PICARONA (skirt ruffle)

ARENDELA (blouse ruffle)

TEMBLEQUE (hairpiece)

MOTA (pom-pom)

CADENA BRUJA (gold chain)

GALLOS (ribbons)

POLLERA (skirt)

GUARDA (area with needlework)

Baseball is popular here. Basketball and boxing are, too. Snorkelers explore the seas. People also love to surf. Some go deep-sea fishing.

There is so much to see in Panama. Do you want to visit?

QUICK FACTS & TOOLS

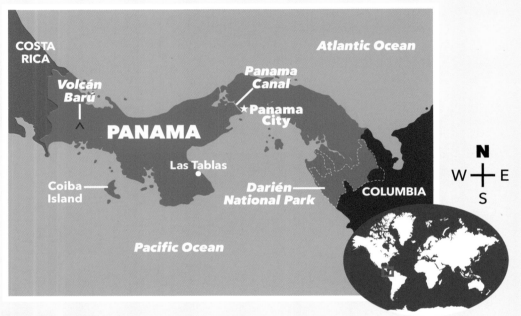

PANAMA

Location: Central America

Size: 29,081 square miles
(75,319 square kilometers)

Population: 4,314,767
(July 2020 estimate)

Capital: Panama City

Type of Government:
presidential republic

Languages: Spanish, English,
indigenous languages

Exports: fruit, nuts, seafood,
iron and steel waste, wood

Currency: balboa,
United States dollar

GLOSSARY

canal: A water-filled channel dug across land so that boats can travel between two bodies of water.

capital: A city where government leaders meet.

climate: The weather typical of a certain place over a long period of time.

crops: Plants grown for food.

festival: A celebration or holiday.

goods: Things that are traded or sold.

isthmus: A narrow strip of land that lies between two bodies of water and connects two larger land masses.

livestock: Animals that are kept or raised on a farm or ranch.

national: Of, having to do with, or shared by a whole nation.

rural: Related to the country and country life.

species: One of the groups into which similar animals and plants are divided.

tropical: Of or having to do with the hot, rainy area of the tropics.

Panama's currency

INDEX

TO LEARN MORE

Finding more information is as easy as 1, 2, 3.

❶ Go to www.factsurfer.com

❷ Enter "Panama" into the search box.

❸ Choose your book to see a list of websites.

FACT SURFER